WORLD EXPLORERS

SIR FRANCIS DRAKE

Kristin Petrie

Checkerboard Library

An Imprint of Abdo Publishing
abdobooks.com

ABDOBOOKS.COM

Published by Abdo Publishing, a division of ABDO, PO Box 398166, Minneapolis, Minnesota 55439. Copyright © 2022 by Abdo Consulting Group, Inc. International copyrights reserved in all countries. No part of this book may be reproduced in any form without written permission from the publisher. Checkerboard Library™ is a trademark and logo of Abdo Publishing.

Printed in the United States of America, North Mankato, Minnesota
102021
012022

Design and Production: Tamara JM Peterson, Mighty Media, Inc.
Editor: Liz Salzmann
Cover Photograph: Ivy Close Images/Alamy Photo
Interior Photographs: Bettmann/Getty Images, p. 15; duncan1890/iStockphoto, pp. 10–11; Everett Collection/Shutterstock Images, p. 13; George-Standen/iStockphoto, p. 26; Historical/Getty Images, pp. 8–9; MicroOne/Shutterstock Images, pp. 16–17; Nastasic/iStockphoto, pp. 19, 28 (top); NoDerog/iStockphoto, pp. 24–25; Stephen Rees/Shutterstock Images, pp. 27, 29 (bottom); Thomas Bowles/Rijksmuseum/Wikimedia Commons, pp. 6–7; vincevoigt/iStockphoto, pp. 5, 28 (bottom); Wikimedia Commons, p. 21; ZU_09/iStockphoto, pp. 20, 22–23, 29 (top)
Design Elements: Joseph Moxon/Flickr (map), Oleg Iatsun/Shutterstock Images (compass rose)

Library of Congress Control Number: 2021942969

Publisher's Cataloging-in-Publication Data
Names: Petrie, Kristin, author.
Title: Sir Francis Drake / by Kristin Petrie
Description: Minneapolis, Minnesota : Abdo Publishing, 2022 | Series: World explorers | Includes online resources and index.
Identifiers: ISBN 9781532197284 (lib. bdg.) | ISBN 9781098219413 (ebook)
Subjects: LCSH: Drake, Francis, approximately 1540-1596--Juvenile literature. | Discovery and exploration--Juvenile literature. | Exploring expeditions--Juvenile literature. | Explorers--Biography--Juvenile literature.
Classification: DDC 970.01--dc23

CONTENTS

SIR FRANCIS DRAKE 4
FRANCIS'S YOUTH 6
SLAVE TRADING 8
NOMBRE DE DIOS 10
ROYAL EXPEDITION 12
SPANISH TERRITORY 14
SIR KNIGHT 18
MORE RAIDING 20
INVINCIBLE ARMADA 22
FALL FROM FAVOR 24
DRAKE'S LEGACY 26
TIMELINE 28
GLOSSARY 30
SAYING IT 31
ONLINE RESOURCES 31
INDEX 32

SIR FRANCIS DRAKE

In the late 1400s, Spaniards first sailed to the West Indies and Central and South America. Over the next decades, they took control of these areas. Spanish armies also conquered the wealthy Aztec and Inca nations and stole their treasures. This made Spain the richest and most powerful country in the world.

Queen Elizabeth I wanted England to have some of Spain's wealth. She encouraged her sea captains to attack Spanish ships and take their cargo. Francis Drake was one of these captains.

Drake sailed around the world, obtaining vast riches along the way. His accomplishments made England wealthy and powerful. He was eventually knighted for his service to England. While some people considered him a thief, others thought of him as a hero.

Drake was called a sea dog. A sea dog was an English captain who attacked Spanish ships.

FRANCIS'S YOUTH

Francis Drake was born around 1540 in Devonshire, England. Francis's father, Edmund, was a tenant farmer and minister. Francis's mother's name is unknown. Francis had 11 younger brothers.

Little is known about Francis's youth. However, he may have been sent to live with William Hawkins in Plymouth, England. Hawkins was one of his parents' cousins.

When Francis was about 13 years old, he became an **apprentice** aboard a trading ship. Francis learned to be a great sailor. When the captain died, he left his ship to Francis. Francis continued to carry freight. But after a few years, he wanted to do something else.

WOULD YOU?

Would you want to leave your family to live with distant relatives? Why do you think Francis Drake was sent to live with Hawkins?

Drake carried freight along the Thames River. It flows through London to the North Sea.

SLAVE TRADING

Drake sold his ship and began working for his cousin John Hawkins. Hawkins was a well-known slave trader. Drake hoped to find adventure while sailing with him.

In 1566, Drake made his first voyage to the New World. Hawkins assigned Drake to one of his slave-trading ships. Drake learned how to navigate the open seas. Hawkins's ships were often attacked, so Drake also experienced his first sea battles.

The following year, Hawkins led a **fleet** on another trading voyage. Drake commanded the ship *Judith*. The fleet sailed to an island off the coast of Mexico. There, Spaniards attacked the English ships. Many of Hawkins's men were killed, and he lost all but two of his ships. Drake would devote the rest of his life to revenge for this attack.

John Hawkins and Drake were involved in slave trading.

NOMBRE DE DIOS

After the attack, Drake returned to England. There, he met a young woman named Mary Newman. In 1569, they married. Drake and Mary did not have any children.

After the wedding, Drake continued his adventures at sea. In 1570, he sailed back to the New World. He **raided** the coastlines and Spanish ports. He found the hidden town of Nombre de Dios, Panama. There, Spanish ships were loaded with gold and silver from mines throughout the New World.

In 1572, Drake again **terrorized** the Spaniards in the New World. He overtook their richest ships and ports, including Nombre de Dios. He collected a great deal of silver and gold.

WOULD YOU?

Would you feel that you had gotten revenge after stealing Spanish treasures? Why do you think Drake continued stealing from the Spaniards?

Drake's fleet often attacked Spanish treasure ships.

11

ROYAL EXPEDITION

Queen Elizabeth was impressed by Drake's accomplishments. She chose him to lead another expedition. It had three main goals. One was to establish trade. Another was to search for a continent in the South Seas. But the most important goal was to gain more Spanish treasure.

Drake's **fleet** had five ships. On December 13, 1577, the *Pelican*, the *Elizabeth*, and the *Marigold* set sail from Plymouth. With them were the *Swan* and the *Benedict*. Both of these ships carried supplies.

The ships crossed the Atlantic Ocean to South America. There, Drake had the *Swan* and the *Benedict* destroyed. They were no longer needed to carry supplies. In August 1578, the remaining ships reached the southern point of South America.

The fleet sailed through the Strait of Magellan. The passage was very difficult. Storms damaged the *Marigold* beyond repair. The *Elizabeth* was blown far out to sea. Only the *Pelican* remained. Drake renamed the *Pelican* the *Golden Hind*.

Queen Elizabeth I of England

SPANISH TERRITORY

After passing through the Strait of Magellan, Drake sailed up the Pacific coast of South America. He was the first Englishman to sail in these waters. Before him, Spaniards were the only Europeans who had been in that area.

The Spaniards did not expect to be attacked and left their harbors unprotected. So, they were easy targets for the English. Drake attacked Spanish settlements and ships and stole their treasure.

Drake continued north. He sailed as far as the 48° north **latitude**. This is near present-day Vancouver, Canada. He then turned south again. He stopped at what is now San Francisco, California. There, Drake claimed the surrounding land for England. He called it New Albion.

WOULD YOU?

Would you go into enemy territory with only one ship? How do you think Drake was able to steal so much treasure?

In California, Drake met the Miwok Native Americans.

SIR KNIGHT

Drake knew Spanish ships would attack him if he sailed back around South America. So instead, he turned his ship west and crossed the Pacific Ocean. He stopped in the Philippines and then made a treaty to trade valuable spices at Moluccas, also known as the Spice Islands. Then, he crossed the Indian Ocean and sailed around the tip of Africa.

Drake reached Plymouth, England, on September 26, 1580. He had sailed around the world! Drake presented Queen Elizabeth with spices, gold, silver, and jewels. For his work, she made Drake a knight in 1581.

For the next few years, Sir Francis Drake spent more time on land than at sea. He was now wealthy and respected. He bought an estate called Buckland Abbey. He was mayor of Plymouth from 1581 to 1584. He was also appointed to England's **parliament**.

Drake's wife, Mary, died in 1583. Two years later, Drake married Elizabeth Sydenham. The couple never had any children.

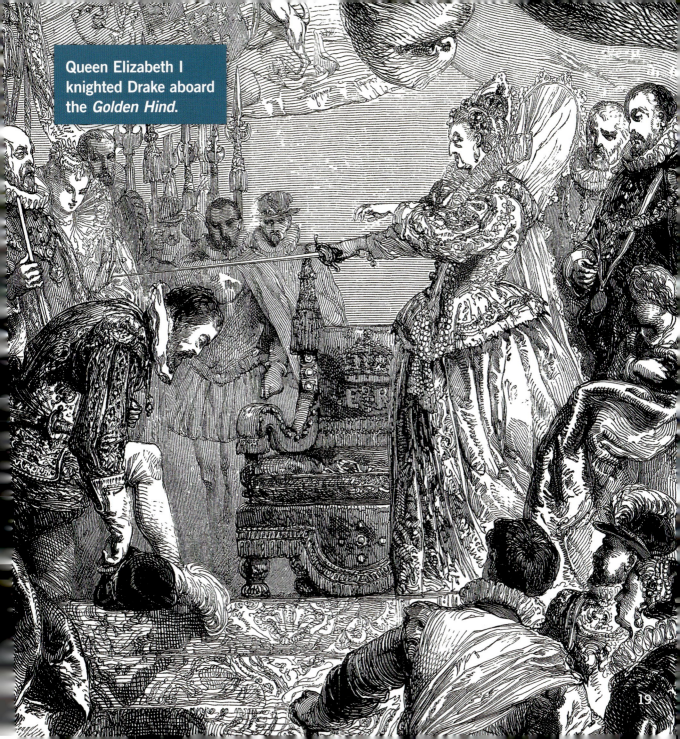

Queen Elizabeth I knighted Drake aboard the *Golden Hind*.

MORE RAIDING

In the fall of 1585, Drake returned to the sea. Queen Elizabeth ordered him to do as much damage to Spain's empire as possible. So, Drake seized its leading settlement, Santo Domingo, on the island of Hispaniola. He also destroyed a fort at St. Augustine, Florida.

King Philip II of Spain was enraged by these attacks. He began planning revenge against the English. In his plan, a large **fleet** called the Invincible Armada would attack the English.

In 1587, Drake was told to stop the Spanish invasion. So, he sailed to Cádiz, Spain. This was where the armada was being prepared. Drake's fleet sank the Spanish ships. Anything Spain could use in the invasion was destroyed or stolen. However, Drake's attack only delayed the Spanish invasion. King Philip became more determined than ever to punish England.

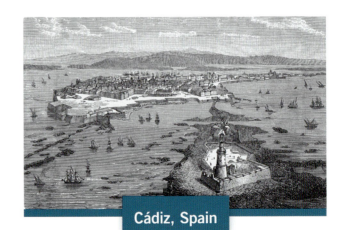
Cádiz, Spain

20

King Philip II of Spain

INVINCIBLE ARMADA

In the spring of 1588, the Spanish armada was finally ready. Nearly 150 warships carried 19,000 soldiers to battle. The English had about 40 warships and many smaller boats. Drake commanded a ship named the *Revenge*.

The **fleets** met in the English Channel in July 1588. The English sent eight ships toward the armada. They were filled with gunpowder and set on fire. To avoid being destroyed, the Spanish ships broke their formation and headed to sea.

The English followed them and the Battle of Gravelines began. The English destroyed or captured many Spanish ships. Thousands of Spanish soldiers died or were taken captive. The remaining Spaniards fled to safer waters. England claimed victory.

The Invincible Armada (*right*) attacked England but was defeated. Fewer than half of its ships returned to Spain.

FALL FROM FAVOR

Drake had defeated the Spanish armada. Nevertheless, he continued to have revenge on his mind. In 1589, Drake headed for a Spanish port in Portugal. He **raided** trading ships but was unable to take over the port.

Queen Elizabeth was disappointed, and she lost interest in her favorite pirate. Back in England, Drake resumed his position in England's **parliament**. He **supervised** the construction of a channel that would bring fresh water to Plymouth. He also dreamed of another attack on Spain.

In 1595, Queen Elizabeth agreed to another raid. Drake sailed with John Hawkins to the New World. By the time the ships reached their **destination**, Drake was the lone commander. Hawkins had died during the voyage across the Atlantic Ocean.

WOULD YOU?

Would you let Drake go raiding again? Why do you think Queen Elizabeth let Drake go on his final voyage?

This map shows European knowledge of North and South America during the late 1500s.

DRAKE'S LEGACY

In the New World, Drake and his crew attacked several Spanish ports. They also took over Nombre de Dios again. By this time, Drake was ill with **dysentery**. But he continued to give orders, even from his deathbed. Sir Francis Drake died on January 28, 1596, off the coast of Panama. The crew buried their captain at sea.

Sir Francis Drake is remembered in good and bad ways. He was a pirate. Yet he gave this wealth to England. He was merciless with his enemies. On the other hand, he was respectful to his crew, and even to his prisoners.

Drake was ambitious and courageous. He was the first Englishman to sail around the world. Along the way, he increased England's influence. Drake helped his country become a world power.

A replica of the *Golden Hind*

There is a statue of Drake in Plymouth, England.

TIMELINE

1566
Drake sails to the New World with John Hawkins.

1570 and 1572
Drake terrorizes the Spanish in the New World.

1581
Drake is knighted by Queen Elizabeth I of England.

1540
Francis Drake is born in Devonshire, England.

1577–1580
Drake sails around the world.

1588

Drake helps England win the Battle of Gravelines against Spain's Invincible Armada.

1596

Sir Francis Drake dies of dysentery on January 28.

GLOSSARY

apprentice—a person who learns a trade or craft from a skilled worker.

destination—the place someone or something is going to.

dysentery—a disease of the intestines.

fleet—a group of ships under one command.

latitude—a measure of distance north and south on Earth's surface. This distance is shown on a map by lines that run parallel to the equator.

parliament—the highest lawmaking body of some governments.

raid—a sudden attack, or to make a sudden attack.

supervise—to watch over and take care of something.

terrorize—to fill with fear and anxiety.

SAYING IT

Cádiz—KAH-deeth

dysentery—DIH-suhn-tehr-ee

Moluccas—moh-LUH-kuhz

Nombre de Dios—NAWM-bray day DEE-ohs

ONLINE RESOURCES

To learn more about Sir Francis Drake, please visit **abdobooklinks.com** or scan this QR code. These links are routinely monitored and updated to provide the most current information available.

INDEX

Africa, 18
Atlantic Ocean, 12, 24
Aztecs, 4

Benedict, 12
birth, 6
Buckland Abbey, 18

California, 14
Canada, 14
Central America, 4
childhood, 6

death, 26

education, 6
Elizabeth, 12
Elizabeth I (queen of England), 4, 12, 18, 20, 24
England, 4, 6, 8, 10, 12, 14, 18, 20, 22, 24, 26
English Channel, 22
Europe, 14

family, 6, 8, 10, 18, 24
Florida, 20

Golden Hind, 12
Gravelines, Battle of, 22

Hawkins, John, 8, 24
Hawkins, William, 6
Hispaniola, 20

Inca, 4
Indian Ocean, 18
Invincible Armada, 20, 22, 24

Judith, 8

knighthood, 4, 18

Marigold, 12
Mexico, 8

New World, 8, 10, 24, 26

Pacific Ocean, 14, 18
Panama, 10, 26
Pelican, 12
Philip II (king of Spain), 20
Philippines, 18
political career, 18, 24
Portugal, 24

Revenge, 22
riches, 4, 10, 12, 14, 18

slavery, 8
South America, 4, 12, 14, 18
Spain, 4, 8, 10, 12, 14, 18, 20, 22, 24, 26
Spice Islands, 18
Strait of Magellan, 12, 14
Swan, 12

trading, 6, 8, 12, 18, 24

West Indies, 4